INı  ...vu

HOW TO GROW GORGEOUS GARDENS INDOORS WITH EASE

Will Cook

Published by TCK Publishing

www.TCKPublishing.com

Get the free newsletter for more healthy weight loss tips:

AuthenticHealthCoaching.com

Why I Wrote This Book

I love gardening! Nothing brings more joy to my heart than to see my new seedlings growing up or harvesting fresh strawberries from my patio garden. I love gorgeous, colorful flowers, growing my own fresh, delicious food, greens, fruits and herbs and growing fun and quirky plants like aloe and other cactuses.

I grow outdoors, indoors, on my patio and balconies and even on rooftops! But I know some people, for whatever reason, can't grow a full garden outside. Maybe you don't have the space, maybe you live in a city apartment or maybe you just don't like weeding and working on your knees all day in the garden. That's okay! You can start a gorgeous garden indoors without all the fuss or hassle. That's why I wrote this book – so that anyone, anywhere in the world can enjoy a wonderful garden in your very own home.

I hope your indoor garden brings you as much joy, happiness and love as writing this book has for me. Happy planting!

Look at those beautiful potted plants! Don't they just make you want to smile?

TABLE OF CONTENTS

Why Start an Indoor Garden?

GARDENING HAS ALWAYS BEEN A POPULAR pastime. it provides great satisfaction, helps relieve stress, and offers an excellent opportunity to exercise daily. Whether you grow flowers, herbs, fruits, or vegetables, your joy will know no bounds when you see your beautiful plants growing before your very eyes. Besides beautifying your home, you will enjoy many benefits from growing an indoor garden.

There are 5 major benefits to starting an indoor garden. They are...

1. Clean Your Environment

This is an especially important aspect for those who live in large cities with high levels of pollution. Your houseplants have the ability to absorb up to 87% of toxins from the air within 24 hours according to NASA! As a result, the air may smell fresher in your home, but even more importantly it will be a lot healthier!

Modern home are filled with toxins including Volatile Organic Compounds (VOCs), formaldehyde (used in construction adhesives), benzene, vinyl chloride and dozens of others. In fact, the EPA lists 33 *"Urban Air Toxics"* on their website (and those are just the ones that have been PROVEN to be toxic by studies).

The point is – your indoor garden will help purify the air you and your family breathes every day and will protect you from many of these household toxins. This is especially important if you live in a city or an area that has a lot of car traffic and exhaust pollution.

2. INCREASE HUMIDITY INDOORS

Growing plants indoors will actually increase humidity and clean oxygen levels indoors considerably. This is an excellent benefit if you live in dry climates. It's also very helpful for people who suffer from air-related allergies or if you are asthmatic. If you live in a very humid climate anyways and find the air is too moist, you can simply use a dehumidifier to control the levels of humidity in your home.

3. BEAUTIFIES YOUR INTERIORS

It goes without saying that any time you see a happy plant you smile inwards. Green plants, lovely flowers, and fruiting plants have that power; they can improve your mood instantly. No matter what plants you choose to grow within your house, they will enhance the beauty and elegance of your home. Your home will smell better, look better, and feel better too!

If you live somewhere where winters are harsh, you can even get a plant that flowers in the winter-time so you can have beautiful flowers all year round. Christmas cactus is a great plant for gorgeous pink winter and white flowers. It's very easy to grow and makes a wonderful dash of color in the winter.

Christmas Cactus blooms all winter long so it will brighten up your home on a dreary winter day.

4. PROVIDE MANY HEALTH BENEFITS

Gardening – both indoors and outdoors – can be extremely therapeutic. Just watching your plants grow can reduce your stress levels, blood pressure and even fight depression. Research studies have shown that people who grow plants enjoy a better disposition, heal better and faster, and have the ability to cope with stress much better.

Studies have also found that children who grow gardens eat more fruits and vegetables, have better social and interpersonal skills, have better attitudes toward education, improved self-efficacy (they're better at setting and achieving goals in life) and more! You can read more about the benefits of gardening for children in the Childrenandnature.org Fact Sheet:

http://www.childrenandnature.org/downloads/CYE factsheet3gardening2009.pdf

5. PROVIDE FRESH AND ORGANIC VEGETABLES, HERBS AND FRUITS

One great advantage you will enjoy from your indoor garden is that you can have fresh vegetables, herbs, and even fruits. There are many vegetables and herbs that can be grown in containers and every time you pluck a veggie from your plants, or use a fresh herb while cooking your heart will sing with joy. You can grow fresh, organic veggies, fruits and herbs all year round!

You can enjoy all these benefits from your indoor garden? Excited? Let's get started!

Chapter 1
What You Need To Start Your Indoor Garden

STARTING AN INDOOR GARDEN CAN BE A LOT easier than you think. You can start anytime with a minimal budget. It doesn't matter how busy you are. Once you start it, you will enjoy the few minutes of work it takes to care for your plants. In fact, most people find this is the best way to relax and get rid of stress and that the routine of watering and tending to your garden becomes a huge source of pleasure.

Here are some helpful tips to help you start your indoor garden in the easiest and most fun way possible:

Start Small

Do not go overboard buying too many potted plants or seedlings. If you're totally new to indoor gardening or gardening in general, having to manage 30 different kinds of plants might be a bit overwhelming. To avoid the stress and work of having to learn about so many different types of plants all at once, just start small. If you're brand new, I recommend starting with 3-5 plants first. It's a good enough number that if you mess up and something dies because you forgot to water it, you'll still have a few plants left. But it's not too many that you get overwhelmed.

You might need to find space for your plants too. That's another great reason why starting small will be a whole lot easier. You can just put the pots near a window or on the window sill and establish a relationship with your plant. You could choose a flower, herb, vegetable or fruit – and see it grow, learn to understand what it requires, how to fight the diseases or parasites that may attack it, what it needs to grow, flower, and/or give fruit. As you gain experience and get used to caring for your plants, you can start to expand your garden gradually until you have all that you can handle and your home can hold.

FOCUS ON WHAT YOU WANT FROM YOUR INDOOR GARDEN

For any lifestyle change (like starting an indoor garden) to be successful you need to have motivation. The stronger the motivation, the faster you will find the road to success and the easier it will be to deal with any changes or challenges that come up in life. When you decide what type of plants you want to grow in your home, think carefully what will give you the most pleasure; what do you want from your indoor garden?

- Do you want gorgeous, colorful flowers that bring a smile to your face all year round?
- Do you want fresh herbs to help you prepare gourmet, healthy meals for your family?
- Do you want cleaner, fresher air?
- Do you want more greenery in your house?
- Do you want to decorate a certain room or spot?
- Do you want something to care for and nurture?
- Do you want to grow fresh vegetables and fruits?

Take out a notebook and write down what you want from your indoor garden. This will help keep you focused and excited about your new project.

Below are some of the most common reasons why people start indoor gardens and how to go about it:

1. A BEAUTIFUL HOME

In this case choose plants that flower, grow colorful foliage, evergreens or even bonsai plants. These types of plants would add color as well as fragrance to your home. They will also enhance the beauty and elegance of your interior décor.

2. A MINI KITCHEN GARDEN

You can very comfortably grow a wide variety of herbs and vegetables in pots. Cooking can be a totally new experience with fresh herbs plucked from your kitchen garden. Think of ripe tomatoes, beans, green peppers, cucumbers, parsley, oregano, basil, strawberry, okra and so on that you could just pluck and use for your cooking.

3. PROVIDE ADEQUATE SPACE AND LIGHT FOR YOUR PLANTS

Before you decide how many pots you will install in your home, check out the space you have available. Keep in mind that you will need to provide enough sunlight to each of your plants. So, even if you will rotate them periodically to occupy the place near your sunny windows, there should enough space for every plant to get enough sunlight.

4. INDOOR GARDENING AIDS

Get in touch with your nearest garden store and/or research on the internet for implements that will make gardening more enjoyable to you and healthier for your plants. Things such as a sunlight lamp, indoor compost maker, exhaust fans, lighting aids, sprays, organic fertilizers and pesticides, pebbles, pots, pot drainers, etc. would help you keep your plants healthy and happy. Remember that different house plants have different requirements for everything from sunlight to water to nutrients (we'll cover that later).

5. USE BEST GRADE POTTING SOIL

It is always best to ask the advice of the shop keeper of your garden store. Buy the best available because it will go a long way. Your local gardening store expert will definitely advise you on what you need to keep your plants healthy and strong. Just make sure you ask someone who has a lot of experience with gardening and not just someone who's working there for a summer job.

Make sure that you follow the instructions with each plant. If you have already decided on which type of plants you want to grow, share these details with the store keeper who could advice you on the exact needs of each plant. If you can't find a local person to answer these questions for you, just search online for "How to take care of a tomato plant" or whatever plant you're growing.

6. GET THE ASSISTANCE OF FARMER'S BEST FRIEND

You cannot imagine the difference a handful of earthworms can do to your plants. You can easily purchase earthworms from the local bait and tackle shop. You can also buy a portable compost maker where you could create your own compost with the help of earthworms and organic waste from your kitchen. This will ensure that you have a perpetual source of high quality fertilized earth for your pots and plants.

If you don't want to deal with the hassle of managing your own earthworms, you can buy fresh compost locally. Always remember that the health of your plants will be determined by the health of the soil they're growing in!

7. WATERING AND MISTING IMPLEMENTS

Watering your plants is one of the most important tasks in the schedule for taking care of your indoor gardening. You will need adequate implements to water your plants; some plants may require regular misting. Also, you will need to research on what type of water your plants would enjoy most. For example, some experts recommend that you use the water in which you have boiled vegetables to water your plants – and your plants will grow very beautifully and healthy (I only recommend this if the vegetables were organic, otherwise pesticides and herbicides could pollute your house plants).

8. FERTILIZER

No matter how good the soil, you may need to add fertilizer at least once in 6 months or one year. I recommend using organic fertilizers or compost as I personally try to avoid chemical fertilizers.

However, it can be a bit more difficult to manage with organic fertilizers. Chemical fertilizers are immediately available for plant uptake, while organic fertilizers are not. Organic Fertilizers need to pass through the gut of microorganisms before they can be broken down into elemental forms that plants can use. Because microorganism populations in containers vary greatly, nutrient delivery may be erratic. Nutrient levels, pH, temperature, moisture levels, soil composition, soil structure and oxygen levels all affect these microorganism populations.

Further, when microorganism populations are low, organic fertilizers tend to build up to much higher concentrations in properly irrigated plants than chemical fertilizers do. If this occurs, when cultural conditions return to favorable, the microorganisms can release large amounts of nitrogen into soils, so it's easily possible to get a delayed nitrogen burn reaction from organic fertilizers - and you may never even realize why it occurred. Because of this, most novice gardeners will want to use chemical fertilizers to start with to make the whole process even easier.

CHAPTER 2
THE BEST TYPES OF PLANTS FOR INDOOR GARDENING

CONTRARY TO COMMON BELIEF, THE LIST OF plants that can be grown indoors is quite varied and long. There are thousands of flowering plants, non-flowering plants, cacti, herbs, fruits, vegetables and even evergreens that you could grow indoors. So, if you love plants and need to grow them indoors take heart in the news that you have plenty to choose from!

One very important thing you should keep in mind while you decide about the number of plants you want inside your home is that indoor plants will raise the degree of humidity in your home. Hence, this is a good thing if you are living in a dry climate, but not so good if it is already humid. So just remember to use a dehumidifier if thinks get too humid with all your new plants.

While it is true that for your plants to live and thrive indoors they should be adaptable to indoor environment – i.e. less light, drier and cooler environment – it is important that you understand that most plants adapt very well indoors if you are willing to go the extra mile to provide them what they need. Plants also respond very well to love – but as a plant lover and gardener, I'm sure you already know that

Here is a very small list of some of my favorite plants you could grow indoors very easily:

1. AFRICAN VIOLETS *(SAINTAPAULIA)*

The African Violets are among the most popular indoor plants because they are as easy to grow as they are beautiful.

Their flowers last quite long and flowers are known to stay in bloom for several weeks when they are cared for well.

TEMPERATURE:

The best temperature for these flowers is 75 degrees Fahrenheit during daytime and about 60-70 at night. They will grow just fine from about 60-80 degrees Fahrenheit (15-27 degrees Celsius).

WATER:

The best way to water these plants is at the roots (pouring water on the plant will spot its leaves so avoid water the leaves!). You could pour water in the plate you place under the flower pot and let the plant suck it up. The water should never be cold. Be careful not to over water your plants; ensure that the container allows for adequate drainage.

SOIL:

It is best to buy ready-made soil mix from your nearest garden store for they will have missed the right proportions of fertilizer in it. African Violets require a fertilizer high in Phosphorous to bloom. In case your plants are not flowering, the problem would most often be that the fertilizer is higher in Nitrogen than Phosphorous.

PROPAGATION:

You can get new plants from leaf cuttings or from the offshoots (plantlets). When the plants produce these offshoots, you need to remove them and plant them in new containers.

2. CROTON *(CODIAEUM VARIEGATUM PICTUM)*

The Croton is a hot favorite indoor plant because of its exceptionally beautiful foliage. It has great color, grows fast and does not require much attention. These plants love sunlight; hence, you would do best to keep them next to sunny south-facing windows (if you live in the north) where they can get direct sunlight for the better part of the day. Plants that do not get enough sunshine will have smaller and less colorful leaves.

A very important thing to keep in mind is that the leaves of this plant are poisonous. If you have small children or pets that might be inclined to chew on the leaves, this plant is not a good choice for you.

TEMPERATURE:

This plant will grow best in environments where the temperature is maintained in the range of 60-80 degrees Fahrenheit (15-27 degrees Celsius).

WATER:

This plant is happy in a high-humidity environment. It requires heavy watering, but you should allow the top soil to dry in between while you mist the leaves once or twice a week. These plants will almost "tell" you how much water they need. If the leaves droop or begin to fall it means it needs more water; if the leaves wilt at the edges, it means you are watering it too much.

SOIL:

The soil for the croton needs to be moist at all times. Too much or too less and the plant suffers. The good news is that it will not take you too long to understand how much water it likes based on how the leaves look; and once you know that you will have little else to worry about.

PROPAGATION:

Crotons are easily propagated by rooting tip cuttings (new growth cuttings) in the spring or summer. For the plants to 'catch' and grow, you will need to maintain a temperature at 70-80 degrees Fahrenheit (21-27 degrees Celsius).

3. CHRISTMAS CACTUS *(SCHLUMBERGERA BRIDESII)*

This plant got its name from the fact that it flowers around Christmas; and the flower is a heart-stopping beautiful pinkish-red. This is one of the most unpretentious plants you can grow indoors. It thrives in cool and dry conditions and does not need too much watering either. It can live well in low light conditions, though it needs bright light for a little part of the day. Too much light will burn the cactus leaves; hence, during bright summer days, it will require shading.

TEMPERATURE:

The Christmas cactus likes a temperature range of 50-65 degrees Fahrenheit. It should not be exposed to direct heat sources (fireplace), vents or the like.

WATER:

The Christmas cactus does not require too much water. However, you need to ensure that the soil is always moist. It is best to keep the pot on a pebble-tray; as the pebbles will absorb water, the plant will get the moisture it requires.

SOIL:

This is one plant that will thrive in any type of soil. Use a good quality potting soil that drains well. For best results you should apply a weak solution of liquid houseplant fertilizer every 2-3 weeks.

PROPAGATION:

Take Y-shaped cuttings from the stem tips and root them for propagation. Mix equal amounts of moist peat and perlite or sand and keep it moist – not wet; wet would rot the cuttings. As soon as the cuttings are rooted, place them in a very loose mixture of good potting soil.

4. ALOE VERA *(ALOE BARBADENSIS)*

These plants are easy to care for, beautiful, and slow growing. They look great in a container and they offer a long list of health benefits as well. Because they are excellent for soothing burns – they are also called popularly 'the burn plants'. Aloe vera is an excellent antiseptic as well and the inside clear flesh can be made into healthy smoothies (just avoid eating the outer green skin because it's a strong diarrhetic).

TEMPERATURE:

Aloe vera requires a temperature range of 50-65 degrees Fahrenheit. It should not be exposed to direct heat sources (fireplace), vents or the like. It requires plenty of sunlight, but not direct sunlight.

WATER:

Water the plant just enough for the soil to remain moist. Allow the top soil dry (1-2 inches). Do not allow the water to sit because the roots of this plant rot easily; water even less during winter months.

SOIL:

Use a well-draining potting mix which is especially used for all types of cacti. It is important that the soil does not waterlog or the roots of the plant will rot. \

PROPAGATION:

You can obtain leaf cuttings for propagation. Cut about 3 inches of the top part of the leaf and allow it to rest for a few days; when the callus is formed at the place of the cut, remove it. Dip it in rooting hormone and bury the cut side in a cacti potting mix. Maintain the soil moist – not wet. The new plants will get roots in 2-3 weeks.

5. GREEN DRACAENA *(DRACAENA DEREMENSIS)*

This is a very beautiful plant with large, long green leaves with white stripes. These plants are unassuming and though they thrive in medium to bright light, they seem just as happy in low light conditions. This is an excellent choice if you are looking for an indoor plant that adds beauty to your home. It can grow 3-10 feet tall with luxuriant upright foliage (most won't exceed 2-3 feet in height).

Be aware that this plant's leaves are poisonous if chewed by children or pets. Hence, if you have either, ensure that they do not have ready access to the plant.

TEMPERATURE:

The Green Dracaena is happiest if the temperature is maintained at 65-75 degrees Fahrenheit. It does not tolerate cold or dry heat.

WATER:

This is a plant that does not require too much watering. Allow the top soil to dry between watering. Water once every 2 to 3 days. Ensure that water never saturates the soil or the leaves will wilt and roots will rot.

SOIL:

Use a well-draining humus-peat-loose soil that does not hold water. Earthworms are excellent helpers in the soil of this plant. Top with fertilizer every 2-3 months. You will need to repot this plant every 2 years. Keep the soil's pH between 6.0 and 6.5.

PROPAGATION:

This plant can be propagated by stem/ tip cutting, air layering or by potting root basal shoots during spring, and/or later summer.

6. GERANIUM *(GERANIUM DISSECTUM)*

These are wonderful flowering plants that come in blue, pink, red and purple with long term continuous flowering. These flowers will grow happily in any soil as long as you do not flood it with too much water. For indoor planting the dwarf variety are the best choices. The plant lives for about 18 months and for the majority of this time they bear lovely flowers.

Geraniums love the sun and hence, require plenty of direct sunlight. This is why these plants thrive best if they are placed on the sill of the window. The plant will start flowering somewhere during mid-summer and will continue flowering until the first winter days. To ensure that it continues to bloom, cut the old blooms as soon as they die.

TEMPERATURE:

For best results, keep the temperature below 70 degrees Fahrenheit for this plant. They can resist the cold very well, but not too much humidity or heat. Keep it away from any direct vents of heat.

WATER:

Geraniums do not like too much water. Keep the soil just a little moist, never soaked. Use pebbles to ensure that the soil drains well. You could water the plant once 2-3 days.

SOIL:

Use compost rich soil if you want the flowers to be happy and flowering throughout the year. Add fertilizer once in a month or two. Geraniums will tolerate poor soil, but in such a case it would not flower as long. For best growth and flowering tenure the plant should feel happy.

PROPAGATION:

For propagation, cut off 3-4 inches of the old plant and bury the cut ends into moist soil. Do not keep the soil wet or in 1-2 weeks the cuttings will root. Transplant the plants in a container during spring.

7. BONSAI PLANTS

Growing bonsai plants is a very satisfying and rewarding hobby. Literally translated as "tray planted" this is an ancient Chinese art, which was perfected by the Japanese. It involves efforts that patiently dwarfs trees and trains them to grow and bear fruit in a tray. You can literally engineer the way the tree grows and looks in the tree, which makes this hobby attractive, relaxing and extremely rewarding.

The dwarf trees will bear dwarf fruits over years of training, which would fill your heart with joy to see. This is not a quick way to grow plants – but extremely rewarding. It takes 3-15 years to grow a bonsai in the desired shape.

TEMPERATURE:

The optimal temperature required by bonsai trees depends from tree to tree. However, the best bet is to keep them in an environment that is between 55-80 degrees Fahrenheit. Bonsai plants love sunlight, so it is best to place them where they get sunlight for the better part of the day. If you cannot offer it enough natural light, use a sunlight lamp.

WATER:

The bonsai trees require everything in minimal quantities; even water. Since they are planted in a tray, you need to take care not to flood them. The soil needs to be mixed with pebbles to ensure proper drainage.

SOIL:

Less is more in this case. The Bonsai trees are systematically dwarfed by cutting roots, and fertilizing it less often than regular indoor plants. Apply fertilizer lightly every 2-3 months. The plant requires pruning and trimming at regular intervals.

PROPAGATION:

The method of propagation depends from tree to tree. Some would propagate from seeds; while some other would propagate from cuttings and/or rootings.

8. SPIDER PLANT *(CHLOROPHYTUM COMOSUM)*

This is one of the most popular plants grown indoors the world over. There are many variants of the plant, which makes it a very attractive option. It has long, thin green leaves with a cream color strip running through its midst. These plants grow up to one foot tall and about 2 feet wide with thick, green foliage. The leaves are long, thin and very beautiful. The baby plants that grow at the end of the stems make the plant look like it holds spiders all around it; hence, its name.

TEMPERATURE:

The Spider Plant is happiest in an environment that stays between 60-80 degrees. It can withstand a little more heat, but not cold. It requires medium sunlight. Hence, if there is too much sunlight in your areas, shade the area.

WATER:

This plant does not require too much water. You will need to keep the soil moist and evenly watered. Too much water and the plant will wilt. Water it once in 2-3 days.

SOIL:

The spider plant requires high quality potting mix soil. Fertilize the soil once in 2-3 months or top it up every month. Ensure that the soil is properly aired and drained.

PROPAGATION:

For propagation remove the plantlets at the end of the stem and pot them in good soil that is maintained with minimum moisture. The baby plants root readily within a week.

9. ENGLISH IVY *(HEDERA HELIX)*

This is a most common outdoor plant in many areas. However, it can adapt very easily indoors as well. It can be grown easily in pot from where it can climb around the room or window. For best effect train the plant into topiary form. It grows fast, can be easily trained and requires very little pampering. Trim it if you want it to stay small. Most people prefer to mold it into wide variety of topiaries.

Beware that this plant's leaves are poisonous; keep children and pets away from this plant.

TEMPERATURE:

This plant grows best in environments that are 55-70 degrees Fahrenheit. This is a sturdy plant that does not respond too well to extreme heat. It loves sunlight but not too much direct light.

WATER:

This plant does not like too much water, but requires it steadily. The best is to always have water in the plate below the pot so it can pull up as much water as it requires. The soil should never become waterlogged.

SOIL:

Use a good potting mix that can drain well. The plant needs water, but it requires the soil to stay moist not wet.

PROPAGATION:

The plant propagates easily through cuttings. Take a few cuttings and bury them in moist soil. You will have roots in a couple of weeks.

10. SNAKE PLANT *(SANSEVIERIA TRIFASCIATA)*

This is a handsome plant that has leaves shaped as long green swords with yellow outline. This plant is so unassuming that many compare it to plastic plants – that is how low attention it demands. It is almost indestructible and hard to kill. It grows to up to 4 feet tall and looks exceptionally beautiful.

TEMPERATURE:

The best temperature for these flowers is 60-80 degrees Fahrenheit and requires low to medium light. However, it does not really complain if it is exposed to high level sunlight or heat.

WATER:

The best way to water these plants is once in 2-3 days for it does not need much watering. It would be good if you let the first 1-2 inches of the soil dry before your watering schedule. Overwatering would lead to root rot.

SOIL:

The plant benefits from using high quality potting mix soil. Fertilize the soil once in 2-3 months or top it up every month. Ensure that the soil is properly aired and drained. Too much water can kill the otherwise very sturdy plant.

PROPAGATION:

You can get new plants from leaf cuttings or from the offshoots (plantlets). When the plants produce these offshoots, you need to remove them and plant them in new containers.

CHAPTER 3
OVERCOMING THE 5 MOST COMMON INDOOR GARDENING PROBLEMS

STARTING YOUR INDOOR GARDEN WILL THROW UP a number of challenges. Of course, the benefits of growing a garden would far outweigh the inconvenience or problems it might generate. The good news is that most of the problems you would encounter can be managed with a little effort and ingenuity.

Here's how to do it!

1. INADEQUATE LIGHT

Most houseplants thrive even in low light with just enough indirect sunlight. However, there are some that require intense and natural light. For this challenge you have two solutions. One is to place the plant near a window or on a window sill. If that is not always possible, use artificial lighting that is available in most garden stores (or order it on the Net).

If you have no spots in your house with lots of natural light, then just focus on growing plants that don't require lots of light.

2. PLANT DISEASES

Plants like all living things are susceptible to a number infections, parasite attacks and diseases. You can solve this challenge by studying carefully about each plant you are growing in your home and learning how to fight each problem that these plants might encounter. Most garden shops will be happy to teach you how to use organic fungicides, pesticides, and other solutions that would help your plants stay healthy. The key here is to make a correct diagnosis as early as possible; especially if you have other plants in your home.

Most diseases can be avoided simply by following the maintenance instructions for each plant and making sure not to over-water or over-fertilize your plants.

3. PROBLEMS WITH HUMIDITY

Some problems require a higher level of humidity to stay alive and happy. This can be a challenge in places where the climate is dry. To overcome this problem, you might like to use room humidifiers or just mist the leaves of the plant as often as it is necessary. Also, it is important that you keep the plants away from places such as heat vents or heaters that can suck the moisture out of the air and harm the plant.

4. UNDER OR OVERUSE OF FERTILIZER

This is a very common problem with new gardeners. It takes a little time to understand what each plant needs.

As a plant lover, you will be delighted to find that each plant has its distinctive needs and if you really love them, you will almost feel what they want – sunlight, fertilizer, and water. You will feel as if they are talking to you and telling you exactly what they want.

When in doubt, you can always contact your local garden store for advice; alternatively there is a lot of information on the Internet just waiting for you to find and use it.

5. INADEQUATE WATERING

It is possible that in the beginning you would be watering your plants too often, too rarely, too much or too less. Too much water can kill a plant just as too less can.

The solution here is learning all you can about your plant and watching closely about signs that it is not happy – such as wilting of tips of the leaves, dropping leaves, yellowing of the leaves, and so on.

A good measure that applies to most plants is to ensure that the soil of the plant is well drained. Unless the containers have proper drainage, your plants will always be in the danger of 'drowning' if too much water gets into the container and there's no way for it to get out.

One very effective method is adding pebbles or rocks to the bottom of the container before adding soil. That will ensure that water drains well while the soil remains moist.

CHAPTER 4
FIGURING OUT WHAT YOUR PLANTS NEED

THERE ARE MANY FACTORS THAT A PLANT requires to grow well and stay healthy. The soil is one of the most important aspects for an indoor plant. Hence, it is very important that each plant has the best soil mix according to its requirement. Generally speaking, most plants would thrive quite well in a good potting mix, which has a 10-10-10 mix of nitrogen-phosphorous-potassium, also known as NPK; but occasionally some plants would require something more such as some plants need phosphorous to grow better and bloom. It is important that you know these little tricks if you want to get the best out of your plants – whether they are flowering plants, herbs, vegetable or fruits.

THE SOIL YOUR PLANTS NEED

A veteran gardener would always mix his own soil. If you are not yet comfortable with the idea, do not worry; you will come to it in a while. This takes time to learn and plenty of experience; so, do not worry if at first you do not seem to understand much about soil and stuff. Stick to the ready-mix potting soils available in the garden store until you are comfortable to try mixing your own soil. There are plenty excellent commercial soils available for potted plants that will do just as well and save you the time and hassle of figuring it out.

Before you give it a try, you will need to learn about what each type of chemical in the fertilizer does and how it would affect your plant.

1. NITROGEN

There are plants – especially those with deep green foliage – that thrive on Nitrogen. The best, in this case, is using the slow-release- fertilizer products. Look for the products that are especially designed for indoor plants. You will need to know at what rate your plant absorbs the fertilizer so you apply just the right amount. Too less or too less, and the plant will wilt.

2. PHOSPHORUS

This is an important ingredient for flowering plants. This will regulate the pH levels of the soil of your indoor plant. The pH is measured on a scale of 0 - 14; 7 - 14 makes the soil alkaline and 6 - 0 makes it acidic. You need to ensure that soil's pH stays in balance. Too acidic will inhibit your plant's ability to absorb phosphorous and hence inhibit its flowering ability.

It is a good idea to have a test kit to keep a close eye on how your soil is doing. This is especially important if you are starting to mix your own soil.

3. POTASSIUM

This is the ingredient that helps your plant to fight diseases and helps it grow healthy fruits fast. There are many liquid fertilizers you can use that will ensure this ingredient is absorbed through the tissue of your plants and keep it healthy. The liquid fertilizers offer you the advantage of being able to add it at a more even rate.

A word of caution when using fertilizers; a newly ready-mix from the garden store will not need fertilizer for a good 6 - 10 months. Talk to your local gardening store experts for advice. Also, never use fertilizer on dry soil as this will saturate it and burn your plant. In fact, in this aspect less is better than more.

CHAPTER 5
STARTING SEEDS INDOORS

STARTING TO GROW YOUR GARDEN RIGHT FROM seed is not only very enjoyable, but also an excellent money-saving way to grow the widest variety of plants. You can always buy seeds from your local garden or online; be sure you check how much time the plant needs to mature and flower or bear fruit. The timing is important for most plants should reach maturity before frost. The flowering plants should reach their maturity about summer when they are supposed to flower.

BUYING SEEDS

It is very important that you buy good quality seeds. Organic seeds and hybrid seeds would be more expensive, but worth the extra cost – especially if you're growing food. I always try to avoid food crop seeds that are not organic due to potential GMO (genetically modified) contamination. You can visit your local garden store or buy from online sites. Most of the seeds you chose will come with easy-to-follow instructions telling you what you need to do and in how much time you should expect your plant to show up.

Do not be tempted to buy large packets of seeds just because they mean less money per seed. Small packets are the best because fresh seed is better than stored ones. It's unlikely you'll grow 30 tomato plants, for example, in your house this year so there's no reason to buy a pack of 100 tomato seeds!

If you think that you can buy in bulk and store your surplus seeds for later use, you may be mistaken. With the passage of time, the stored seeds will have lesser and lesser capacity to germinate. It is okay though to store the excess seeds for next year planting; but ideally you should not store seeds for much longer than a year, especially if you're new at seed storing. Some seeds save much longer than others. For example, most lettuces will last around 6 years whereas parsley and onions often only last 1 year.

SEED CONTAINERS

There are so many types of containers that are specially designed for seedlings. This means that instead of potting all seeds in one container, you can have one seed per tiny container in an ice-tray type container. These honeycomb trays come in various sizes so you could choose the right one for the type of plant you are planning to grow. For example, you will need large trays for leaks or onions, but smaller trays for pansies or begonias.

You can always reuse the seed trays since they are made of plastic and can last for a long time. However, be careful to sterilize these trays before every use by soaking the cleaned cups in a solution of bleach or other disinfectant for 30 minutes, then rinse and use. Mix the solution to the strength recommended on the label for disinfecting surfaces.

You could also use containers from organic materials such as shredded wood, newspaper, and the like. These are especially good for seedlings that do not fare too well after transplantation.

You could also use clear plastic domes that fit over trays of plants. These domes will allow light in, but will at the time prevent moisture from escaping. They can also help retain heat provided to the root zone. Obviously, the domes have to be removed when the seedlings are tall enough to touch them, otherwise your plants will suffer.

TIMING

As mentioned earlier, timing is very important when you plan to start your seeding indoors. Check the table on the next pages for a general idea:

TYPE OF PLANT	MONTH	TIME OF INDOOR GROWTH
Lisianthus.	Mid January	16-17 weeks
Geraniums, wax begonias, pansies/violas, leeks, onions.	Early February	14-15 weeks
Browallia, clarkia*, dusty miller, impatiens, larkspur, stocks, torenia, fountain grass, lobelia, nemesia*, celery.	Mid February	12-13 weeks
Ageratum, coleus, dahlia, gazania, heliotrope, lavatera*, petunias, rudbeckia (black-eyed susan), scabiosa, schizanthus, snapdragons, verbena, vinca/periwinkle, broccoli, cabbage, cauliflower, head lettuce.	Early March	10-11 weeks
Bells of ireland, candytuft, cleome, dianthus/pinks, hollyhock, marigold (African), melampodium, mimulus, nicotiana, nierembergia, ornamental pepper, annual phlox, salpiglosis, scarlet sage/salvia, statice, strawflower, sweet alyssum, tithonia, trachymene, peppers, eggplant.	Mid March	9 weeks

TYPE OF PLANT	MONTH	TIME OF INDOOR GROWTH
Amaranthus, aster, baby's breath, bachelor buttons, balsam, calendula, celosia, cornflower, four o'clock, marigold (French and gem), morning glory, nasturtium, ornamental basil, ornamental kale, portulaca, strawflower, tomatoes.	Early April	5-6 weeks
Cosmos, sweet peas, thunbergia, zinnia.	Mid April	3-4 weeks

* These plants are best to grown in biodegradable containers for they do not fare too well when transplanted.

TYPE OF SOIL

In most cases the commercial mixes for seeding are the best to use. These usually contain no soil; they are a mix of vermiculite and peat and are sterile. These types of mixes are the best for your seedlings – especially if you are new to gardening.

The advantage of this mix is that it is light, free from any type of disease or weeds and is just porous enough to ensure that your seeds germinate in optimum time.

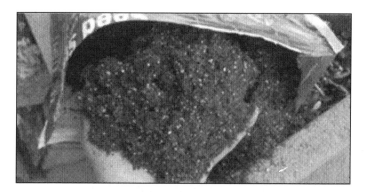

A mix of vermiculite and peat in a typical commercial soil mix available at every gardening store or online.

Take the trays with the small seedling cells, fill them with this mix and pour water over them before you put in the seeds. After adding water the mix will shrink. Keep adding and mixing with water until the tray is full and the mix is comfortably moist.

Read carefully the instructions on the seed package. It would be mentioned there how deep the seed should be planted for best results. If it is not mentioned, use the standard rule, i.e. plant the seed just deep enough that you could have three other seeds planted right on the top of it. Remember to mark each container with what type of plant it carries.

Some seeds might need light to germinate. These seeds should be buried too deep in the mix. Rather you place them on the seeding mix and cover them with a light layer of vermiculite. This will allow light and ensure that the seed will grow well.

When and if you are using old seeds, plant more than one in the container for all might not germinate and you do not want to lose time with dead seeds.

IDEAL PLANTING LOCATION

Contrary to common belief, the window is actually NOT the best place to germinate your seeds. This because the window sill will have all the extremes – too much light, too much heat (during the day time), too much cold (during the night time), etc. For seeds to germinate well, they need warmth and moisture. Too cold or too hot will damage the seed and affect the germination rate.

Even if every other aspect (such as heat and moisture) are controlled on the window sill, you will still risk growing bent plants for they tend to grow towards the light and you would not want that from your plants. Too much water will also damage your seeds; so, be careful with the watering aspect as well.

Choose a place where temperature is consistent at about 60 degrees Fahrenheit and has no drafts, excessive heat or cold. Protect your seeding trays from pets, children and spills. To provide it with the light that the seed requires, you can use grow lights. If you do not have access to these specialized lights or can't afford them, you can make your own with the help of white and natural daylight tubes or two 'cool white' fluorescent tubes. These will ensure that the seeds get just enough light. Remember the light should be just above, preferably at a height of 2-4 inches above the tray. Keep the light on for about 12-16 hours.

One other very important aspect that contributes to the healthy germination of your seeds is the heat at the bottom of the seed tray. Owing to the moisture content the temperature could drop by at least 5 degrees Fahrenheit. To ensure that temperature stays comfortable, use special heating mats designed for this purpose.

A word of caution – if you are using a timer for the lights you installed above the seedlings, do not plug the heat mats into the same source.

WATER AND FERTILIZER

The potting mix should be maintained moist for the seeds to germinate well. The best is to use a gentle spray to add water daily. However, you could also add water carefully while ensure that the mix is drained well. You do not want to rot the seeds.

You do not need to fertilize the potting mix; the readymade potting mix has all it needs. However, once the seedling has acquired a few leaves, it will be good to add a weak general purpose water-soluble fertilizer mixed one-fourth strength every week. Add water as required for the rest of the week.

TRANSPLANTING TIME

Once the seedling is strong enough with leaves and a strong upright stem, it is time to move it into its own container. You still need to mark it for it is yet to look anything like the mature plant it is intended to be.

Lift seedlings by the root-ball, using a spoon or plant tag for support if necessary. Never hold the seedling by its stem, as you may crush it, or harm the growing tip. Crushing a leaf does not matter much for the plant will soon get a new leaf; however, if the stem is damaged, your plant might die or grow badly and you do not want that.

Chapter 6
Playing God – How To Control The Climate For Your Indoor Garden

There are three major aspects that would control the climate necessary for your indoor gardening: (1) temperature, (2) lighting, and (3) humidity. Each one of these aspects is critical to the life of your plants and their development. It may look and sound very complicated to ensure the perfect climate for your plants, but it is not. Of course, you need to initially research the plants you plant to grow and their requirements. Once you have that down, regulating indoor climate is not that difficult with the modern appliances available today.

Temperature

Most plants are happy with a temperature of 65-75 degrees Fahrenheit. Plants consume more energy when the temperature is warm than when it is cold. They will definitely adapt to a cooler room – for example rooms with air conditioner - but it will stress out the plants because they need warm temperature in the daytime and cool at night.

Air conditioning (making the room cold in the day time) would confuse the plant and interfere with its ability to carry out photosynthesis. The plant will start photosynthesis at night (when the temperature rises) and there will be no light to help it produce food. The result will be a sick plant which will soon die if the climate is not corrected. It's okay to run your air conditioning if you have house plants in the summer! Just make sure that it's not below 65 degrees and that your plants aren't directly underneath a cold vent.

For best results you should provide at least a 10 degree fall in temperature at night (this will most likely happen naturally unless you're running air conditioning 24/7). Pay special attention to this aspect in the summer when the temperatures tend to remain high even at night. If the climate is not corrected, the plants will drop leaves, fade and die; even if all other aspects are perfect.

To ensure that your plants are happy, arrange them in groups according to their temperature, humidity and light requirements. This will save you a lot of effort, and money by managing the climate with what you already have rather than of trying to make drastic changes that would actually work against the natural rhythm of your environment at home.

LIGHTING UP YOUR INDOOR GARDEN

Light is a vital pre-requisite for an indoor garden as it helps the plant to produce chlorophyll through photosynthesis. This is the process of making food – the process of advanced life on Earth itself. It's also the process which will keep the plant looking healthy, green and beautiful. Nothing manmade can replace the intensity of sunlight; however, there are the HID (high intensity discharge) lights, which can do an excellent job keeping your sun-loving plants happy.

If you do it right, your African Violets, orchids, citrus and hibiscus plants will flower and look bright and green throughout the year. This is no small achievement; the key is, 'doing it right'.

THE RIGHT COLOR OF LIGHT

Sunlight offers the complete spectrum of light and plants use it all in the process of photosynthesis. However, the red and blue lights were found the most critical to their growth and positive photosynthesis (light that makes plants grow towards it). Blue light regulates plant growth and is especially beneficial for growing plants with foliage.

THE RIGHT INTENSITY

You will need to regulate the intensity of the light to ensure that your plants receive the right amount necessary for their growth. Plants react differently to color of light as they do to the intensity of light. Most plants do well in light that is kept about 1-3 feet away. Flowering plants are happier when the intensity of light is high – say 10-12 inches away, while foliage plants are okay with the light some 36 inches away.

Each plant has its own requirements. The trick is to group like-type plants together so you could provide the right type and amount of light to them better. When you design your indoor garden keep in mind, which plants want what and group them accordingly. Unless this is done right, you will have some plants happy and some wilting away – and you do not want that.

To find out what each one of your plants needs, you might like to research on the Internet about each one and note all the requirements where you can refer to them every once in a while. You can also do it through trial and error; plants have a way to "tell" you that they are not happy. Look for telltale signs such as wilting of leaves, drooping leaves, yellowing of leaves, etc. The change comes pretty fast within a few days; so you can know for sure what the plant likes and dislikes. Adjust the light to the intensity it likes; you will know when you hit the right combination for your plant will look as beautiful as it would be out in the sunlight.

THE RIGHT DURATION

All plants can be divided into three major groups:

1. Short-Day Plants – in this category are the plants that will need less than 10 hours of light. In this group are plants such as azaleas, chrysanthemums, begonias, and kalanchoe. For these types of plants to flower you need to provide about 10 hours of direct light.

2. Long-Day Plants – in this category are plants that require a minimum of 14-18 hours of light. In the group you will find the majority of garden flowers and most vegetables. When the light is inadequate these plants yellow and droop.

3. Day-Neutral Plants – in this category you will find foliage plants, coleus, African violets, geraniums – these are plants that require about 8-12 hours of light throughout the year.

THE IMPLEMENTS

There are all kinds of light specially designed for indoor gardening whether this is for starter seedlings, flowering plants, or green foliage. There are many types of lights available and each type caters to a particular aspect of growing a healthy indoor garden. You will need to mix and match to ensure that your indoor garden gets what it needs best.

1. Incandescent Lights – this type of light is perfect for lighting a room where low-light plants are grown such as dracaenas, ferns and vines. These lights will give plenty of heat (10% light and 90% heat); hence, are not suitable for most plants unless they are cacti, tropical plants or succulents.

2. Fluorescent Light – this type of light is best for day-neutral plants that require low-medium light such as vegetables and African Violets. The lights come in the form of tube-like bulbs in various sizes (T12, T8 and T5). The thinner the bulb, the brighter the light it provides would be. They provide full spectrum light and use 75% less energy than the incandescent lights. They provide 6500 Kelvin light when most indoor plants require 4000-6000 Kelvin degrees.

With this type of light you could emulate the conditions required to grow all types of herbs, starter seedlings, greens, orchids, succulents, and so on. These plants perform well when exposed to the full spectrum lights fluorescent bulbs provide. The T5 and T8 bulbs placed at about 2-4 inches away emulates sunlight and are excellent for germinating seeds. For grown up plants the plants will benefit if they are kept 1-2 feet away from the light source.

3. Compact Fluorescent Lights - These are the lights you would like to use for your indoor garden not only because they are the best suited, but also because they cost a fraction of what the incandescent lights do. To ensure to get it right (and not waste your money with changing the lights often) ask a specialist to help.

POINTS TO KEEP IN MIND ABOUT LIGHTING

Do not worry too much about finding the right lighting for your garden. It is easier than it looks. Consult a specialist in the beginning and afterwards you play it by the ear. You will find your plants have a way to tell you what they need. Every gardener will swear that they can tune in into what they plants need. What is left, you will learn with experience. Give yourself about 6-12 months and you will know that there is to know about the plants you are growing. In the meantime, you will need to keep in mind certain important things about lighting:

1. Plants Need Darkness, Too

All plants – even the ones that love the highest intensity of light – need a period of darkness. They take rest during this time and respirate (take in oxygen and give out CO2), which is a very important part of their growth process. This will influence the rate of their growth, flower and fruit bearing abilities as well.

2. Keep Lighting Even

You will need to rotate the plants each week preferably, though you can do once or twice a month as well. The centre of the bulb will provide the highest intensity of light (and heat) and hence, rotating the plant will ensure that the whole plant is exposed to light equally.

3. Proper Maintenance of Fluorescent Lights

When the ends of the tube darken, the bulbs/ tubes need to be replaced. A spent up tube/ bulb will give much less light than it is designed to do. Unless it is replaced in time, the plants would suffer.

You will also need to clean the surface of the tube/ bulb regularly for dust would also diminish the intensity of light that it transmits.

4. Check the Heat Level

Do you know a great way to find out whether the light arrangement you are providing is okay with the plants or not? Just place your hand above the plants that are provided light; if you feel any heat, then the light is too close. Move it away until your hands do not feel any difference in terms of heat.

AIR CIRCULATION AND INDOOR GARDENING

Without proper air circulation you can never have a perfect garden. Stagnant air over-heat and creates conducive atmosphere for pests to grow. This is why you should never overcrowd the indoor garden area; nor should you allow foliage to touch.

You need to control air circulation if you want your garden to prosper. Keep in mind that any type of light arrangement – which is vital to the healthy growth of your indoor garden – will generate heat. The best way is to let fresh air in at regular intervals. If you do this, you would hardly need any additional system to regular your air circulation. However, this might not always be possible for various reasons.

There are many ways to control your environment among which, two are very popular and easy:

1. Intake and Exhaust System

You may like to consider installing intake-exhaust systems that will ensure proper air circulation in your home and provide your plants the much required "fresh air". These systems are able to reduce the temperature and with the help of circulation fans you would be able to control your environment with relative ease.

2. Air Conditioning Systems

This is even easier than the intake-exhaust systems for everything is automated, i.e. temperature, humidity; and it even has an automatic cut off. Most people prefer air conditioning, because it is easier to set and monitor and it feels better, especially in climates where heat and humidity are high.

No matter what system you use, keep in mind that your plants would still need fresh air. Hence, you should at least 3-4 times a week leave your windows open to let the sun and fresh air in. If you can do it daily, it would be ideal.

You are aware that absence of CO2 can sabotage the growth of your plants, no matter how perfect everything else is. If your CO2 level is too low, your plants cannot create photosynthesis. To avoid this problem, you need to add a CO2 generator and meter to your indoor garden as well. Ignoring this important element in their environment will create plenty of problems with the flowering, growth and looks of your plants.

HUMIDITY CONTROL AND INDOOR GARDENING

After the temperature and air circulation, humidity is the most important aspect that requires regulation to ensure a healthy and beautiful indoor garden. Plants adapt well, but there are certain elements that they need to be perfect. Humidity is one of these aspects. If it is too humid or too dry, they stop the photosynthesis process, which results in malfunction in the absorption of nutrients. This in turn, would interfere with the ability of the plant to take in water and carbon dioxide (CO_2) – which will result in a very sick plant.

Also, in the dark, a poor humidity control is likely to lead to mold formation, pest infestation and diseases setting in. Without proper control of the humidity, plants cannot be or look healthy no matter what you do for your garden. You need to get it right.

Install a humidity meter in your home, especially in the places where you keep your plants. This meter will tell you whether or not you need to intervene to maintain the optimal humidity levels for your plants. Use a humidifier or de-humidifier as the case may be to ensure that you create the proper ambiance for your plants to thrive.

CHAPTER 7
PROTECTING YOUR GARDEN FROM PESTS AND DISEASE

YOUR BEAUTIFUL INDOOR GARDEN WILL NOT BE perfect no matter what you do. But that is what will make you love it even more. While you will not have any weeds to worry about, there would be plenty to worry about with pests. If you are lucky, you will be able to prevent most pest attacks. But, in most cases you should be able to counter the problem with a little timely intervention.

PREVENTION IS THE KEY

Prevention is indeed your best option and hence, you will need to focus on this aspect most. Take these few steps and mostly likely, you would not have much trouble with your indoor garden:

1. PULL OUT ANY WEAK PLANTS

If you find that there are weak, wilted plants – and there is no apparent reason - they may be infected or under pest attack. Even if they are not, they are red flags for pests. Pull them out and dispose of them immediately. If possible – and if you are in doubt – quarantine the plant where it is not connected to the rest of your plants so you could observe it.

2. USE READYMADE POTTING MIX

The readymade potting mix soils that you buy at the garden stores are disinfected and hence healthy. These soils are not likely to carry any disease or eggs of pests that could in the future attack your plants. Alternatively, you may use self-made organic composting methods, mulching and top-dressing of your soil with compost or natural fertilizer to grow healthy and vigorous plants.

3. SEAWEED MULCH OR SPRAY

Seaweed is a natural pest preventive; it also contains a number of trace elements such as barium, iron, calcium, zinc, sulfur and magnesium, which would ensure best growth in your plants. You may use seaweed fertilizer in mulch or spray form to ensure good growth and ensure that your plants have enough strength to resist disease.

4. MINIMIZE INSECT HABITAT

Keep the area where your indoor garden is clean for any type of dirt can easily become a breeding place for plant pests. Always use clean mulch.

5. KEEP FOLIAGE DRY

As much as possible, try keeping the foliage of your plants dry. Wet foliage attracts insects and fungus formation which will damage your plants.

6. DISINFECT

Every time you touch a sick plant disinfect your hands before touching a healthy one. You also need to disinfect all your tools if you found any of your plants under attack of pests or any disease. This will prevent spreading the problem to other healthy plants.

THREE MOST COMMON PESTS IN INDOOR GARDENS

There are many pests out there, but the good thing about indoor gardens is that you would be able to leave most of them outside. Nonetheless, there are a few which would be able to get to your garden indoors, too.

Here are the three most common among these:

I. MITES

There are three types of mites that are commonly found in indoor gardens and these are spider mites, spotted mites and black mites. The mites are very small pests, but are powerful and very harmful for they live in colonies. These are in fact, one of the worst types of indoor garden pests. If they find the conditions suitable, you will have over 10,000 mites from just 10 in less than a month. Mites kill the plants by sucking their sap; they bite into veins of the leaves, mostly on the underside where they cannot be seen easily. As it is, they are so tiny in size that it is very difficult to see them until the plant shows symptoms of sickness.

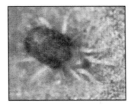

Closeup photo of a mite pest.

The attacked leaves will have tiny dots on their underside if you care to look closely. Use magnifying glass when you are in doubt so you could make a correct diagnosis. Start your inspection by checking the undersides of the leaves; that is where they would colonize.

2. THRIPS

Like mites, thrips too are so tiny that they are almost impossible to identify with the naked eye. This is why in most cases they go unnoticed until the plant wilts. Like mites, thrips too are sap-suckers. An important telltale sign is the shiny deposit they leave on the leaves of the plants. Unlike mites, which have a round shape, thrips are oval; they look just like a grain of rice. A good thing about these pests is that they do not multiply as fast as the mites do.

3. Fungus Gnats

An adult fungus gnat.

This insect is quite visible, even though it is small in size. It is easy to notice them because they would be flying around here and there. At the first glance, they appear to be totally black. It is important to know that this pest spends the first part of its life inside the soil.

A fungus gnat larva.

The gnat larvae's first source of food is the roots of your plants, and other organic matter they find inside the soil. This is why it is disinfected and made sterile before you pot your plants. Fortunately, the fungus gnats are happier with hydroponics than with soil. As soon as they mature into flying adults, they start laying more eggs in your soil and very soon you will have an epidemic on your hands if you do not check it in time.

HOMEMADE REMEDIES FOR PEST CONTROL

The best way to fight pest infestations is with organic pesticides, which you can buy from your garden stores. Alternatively you can use some very simple to make yet very effective homemade pest control formulas!

1. FOR MITES, APHIDS AND MEALY BUGS)

Mix two teaspoons of canola oil (4 teaspoons of cayenne pepper or hot pepper sauce) and 4-5 drops of

Dr. Bronner's soap into a quart of water. Put the mix into a spray bottle shake well and spray on the underside of the leaves of the plant. Remember, the mites live mostly underneath the leaves.

2. FOR MILDEW

Mix water and milk in equal proportions. Pour in a spray bottle and spray it on the affected plant 3-4 times weekly.

3. FOR FUNGUS AND OTHER INSECTS

Mix 4 teaspoons of baking soda into a quart of water and spray the mix on the plant every alternate day.

Make a mix with two teaspoons of cooking oil, 4 teaspoons of baking soda, 4-5 drops of Dr. Bronner's plain soap and a quart of water. Spray the affected plant every 2-3 days.

4. FOR MITES, GNATS AND MOST OTHER PREDATORY INSECTS

This is one of the drastic yet very effective methods to counter the pest problem. Buy predatory nematodes (quite inexpensive) and transfer them to your plants through watering it over the plants. Once they reach the soil, these predatory nematodes will kill all the thrip, mites, larvae, and gnats they find.

Diatomaceous Earth is another thing you could use to fight infestation of pests. This is a mix of silica dioxide, which – if you look at it under microscope – looks like razor blades. What you need to do is dust the leaves of your plants with this mix. Make sure to wet the leaves a little so the dust will stick properly. When the pests would want to bite, they would cut themselves and die.

Preventing Fungus and Mold in Your Indoor Garden

Fungi are wonderful organisms and they're responsible for most of life on Earth (there would be no soil without the fungi!). But certain types of fungi can infect your garden above the soil (this is known as foliar fungus) and below the soil (this is known as soil born fungus). The best way to control fungus is prevention. However, when fungus and mold gets out of control you can treat it with a good organic fungicide.

1. Foliar Fungus

This type of fungus will attack the leaves and stems of a plant. They will appear as dark spots or splotches on the foliage. These forms of fungus are common when you use cold water to water your plants. It is best to use warm (tepid) water for your plants especially when you are misting the leaves of your plants. It can also be caused when the humidity crosses over 60%. You will know that your plants are affected by the dark spots that appear on the leaves.

To prevent it from forming, use tepid water for your plants and keep a close eye on the hygrometer (apparatus to measure humidity). Also, install a vent fan to encourage air circulation and dissipate excess moisture in the air.

If the plant is already under attack, remove all the infected leaves immediately. Then, use an organic fungicide every 3-4 days until you are sure that your plants are safe and recovering.

2. SOIL BORN FUNGUS

This type of fungus will attack the roots of your plant and it will be visible on the surface of the soil in the initial stages. These types of fungus, like all others, proliferate when there's too much moisture. This often happens if the soil is retaining too much water retention owing to improper drainage. Sometimes, you may get an infected planting medium when you buy a potted plant or the soil may be infected as well.

To prevent soil born fungus you need to use sterile planting medium, and ensure proper drainage of the soil with the help of drainage holes at the bottom of the container and maintaining proper soil texture.

If the plant is under attack in spite of the preventive measures, use a biodegradable soap solution for the soil (1 oz Dr. Bronner's soap with 15 oz of water is what I use). The fungus would die after 3-5 applications. Ensure that you mix the fungicide as per the instructions and the drainage is proper.

CHAPTER 8
INDOOR GARDEN DESIGN IDEAS

THERE ARE MANY WAYS TO BRING IN THE outdoors inside. The sky is the limit when it comes to choosing designs and ways to arrange your lovely potted plants around your home. Each home is unique and as is its interior décor and its owner's taste. So there is no hard and fast rule; you can design it to please your eye. To inspire you, here are a few suggestions:

A WALL OF GREEN PLANTS

You can create a beautiful live wall with a simple metal rack and a number of foliage plants to fill it. This will help you focus your light on the plants and also create a stunning effect in the room. To sustain it lively and green, you need to focus on the intensity of light, humidity levels and be careful that pests don't get to it. Rotate the plants from time to time so they are exposed to light evenly and you will have something that everyone who comes to your home would admire.

There are many styles in which you could implement this idea. Here are some examples, but you could try various other arrangements depending upon your home interior décor, plants you love and the amount of money you want to invest in supporting implements such as lighting and the plant holders, etc.

FERN GARDEN

Ferns are very beautiful, hardy plants that will grow well wherever you place them. They require little light and do not need much watering either.

Try placing large pots in a typical arrangement to create a fern forest or place them all over the room. Their rich green color and splendid foliage would enhance your mood 24x7 and your room will look more inviting.

Ferns are also excellent plants for cleaning the air and they're one of the reasons why the air in a rainforest smells so good!

CACTUS GARDEN

A cactus garden is one of the most beautiful types you can have indoors.

Cacti are among the most unpretentious plants and you will, with very little effort, have a most beautiful garden with the least of effort.

BONSAI GARDEN

The bonsai garden is not for amateurs. This is something you nurture for years before it takes the shape you plan – but in the end it would make your heart sing literally.

You can make the most exquisite designs with the bonsai trees – provided you have the time and patience to build it. It takes about 5-15 years to have a proper bonsai garden.

If you are looking for a short-cut you could buy bonsai trees and replant them in the indoor landscape you have in mind. However, the trees do not come cheap so, you should be prepared to invest a small fortune if you intend to go this way.

JAPANESE GARDEN

The Japanese Garden may be unparalleled in its beauty. There are plenty of resources on the Net that will teach you how to design a Japanese garden indoors. The most attractive part of this type of garden is that it would have to be around a body of water like a mini pond or fountain.

It takes a lot of ingenuity and creativity to make a veritable Japanese garden. It has beauty in its asymmetry and is most natural looking even though it is manmade. The beauty of this garden is that it demands that you (the creator) imitate Mother Nature in its elements and arrangements.

TERRARIUMS

This is the latest in indoor gardening today. Once upon a time you would have found this only as school projects; today it is the ultimate in creativity.

You can have them open or closed – and the challenge lies in creating a complete ecosystem based on a theme of your choice – i.e. a miniature complete garden.

VERTICAL AEROPONICS TOWERS

If you want to grow food and have never heard of aeroponics before, you're in for a treat.

This is an awesome way to grow fresh food at home, indoors, outdoors or even on rooftops. There are so many great advantages of growing an aeroponics garden.

First of all, aeroponics gardening uses absolutely no soil, meaning you don't have to deal with weeding, fertilizers or soil management. Secondly, aeroponics systems use only about 10% of the water compared to traditional gardens. All the water in the system is recycled so there's no runoff which is why you can grow plants with much less water than traditional gardening. With aeroponics the plants also grow much faster as well (NASA quoted that plants in aeroponic systems grow at least twice as fast as soil gardens).

Aeroponics can be used to grow almost anything, including herbs, fruits, vegetables and flowers. These systems can be placed in small spaces, such as decks, balconies, rooftops, porches and patios and indoors near windows.

There are different types of systems available, big and small. You can also try making the system yourself. These systems pretty much resemble a tower. Some people use nothing more than a sealable storage bin, fittings and PVC pipes (just be warned that PVC will leach phthalates and other toxic chemicals into the plants – which is why I never use it for gardening). A pump is also needed to recycle and deliver the water for your irrigation system.

Aeroponics gardens require weekly maintenance that consists of adding water to the reservoir and testing the water/nutrient solution pH to make sure it's in an acceptable range (5 to 7 is required for the plants to absorb nutrients from the water).

This chef in New York City grows all his produce fresh on the rooftop of his restaurant with about 30 Vertical Tower Garden units.

Learn more about vertical aeroponics gardens on our Facebook page here:

http://on.fb.me/HmllNU

FANCY DESIGNS

There are so many designs today to choose from. Here are some examples that would give you a broad idea. Often just watching something beautiful can inspire you to create a masterpiece of your own. Use these images to unleash your imagination and create your own indoor gardens.

A container garden pyramid!

A fancy growing system using grow lights.

A gorgeous terrarium design.

A fun and creative design piece.

Hanging wall pots – even better than a painting to decorate your wall!

A great centerpiece for a dining table.

Like a trophy room for your plants!

Dazzling hanging terrariums

ABOUT THE AUTHOR

Will Cook is the bestselling author of *Urban Gardening* and *Indoor Gardening* Will is an avid gardener and loves growing his own fresh food on his balcony. Will believes the world would be a better place if everyone cared for a few plants and grew their own food (even if it's just a little bit).

Connect with Will on Facebook at:

http://on.fb.me/HmllNU

RECOMMENDED BOOKS ON GARDENING AND SUSTAINABILITY

Urban Gardening: How To Grow Food In Any City Apartment Or Yard No Matter How Small

This is a fantastic book for anyone in the city who wants to grow a fabulous urban garden.

The Vertical Gardening Guidebook: How To Create Beautiful Vertical Gardens, Container Gardens and Aeroponic Vertical Tower Gardens at Home

This is a great book for anyone interested in learning how to grow vertical gardens which allow you to grow more food in less space.

Indoor Gardening: How To Grow Gorgeous Gardens Indoors With Ease

This book is perfect for anyone who wants to grow an indoor garden for food, fun, or just to create a gorgeous ambiance in your home. Did you know that some plants can remove as much as 87% of the toxins in your home in just 24 hours?

Container Gardening: How To Grow Food, Flowers and Fun At Home

This book is great if you want to create gorgeous, fun, container gardens at home including detailed instructions for terrariums, growing succulents, bonsais, and other fun and unique plants.

Chicken Raising 101: How To Raise Chickens In Your Backyard for Eggs, Fun and Profit

This is a wonderful guide to raising your own chickens at home. If you've always wanted your own chickens but don't know how to do it right, this book is for you!

Greenhouse Gardening 101: How To Build Your Own Greenhouse for Growing Vegetables, Fruits, Herbs and Food

Greenhouse Gardening 101 is a great guide for anyone who wants to learn how to build their own greenhouse in the backyard

Natural Mosquito Control: How To Get Rid Of Mosquitos Fast Without Toxic Chemicals or Insecticides

Natural Mosquito Control is the complete guide to killing and repelling mosquitoes without any pesticides or toxic chemicals!

Made in the USA
San Bernardino, CA
14 September 2018